Weather

KINGFISHER
LONDON & NEW YORK

First published as *Kingfisher Young Knowledge: Weather* in 2006
Additional material produced for Macmillan Children's Books by Discovery Books Ltd.
Library of Congress Cataloging-in-Publication data has been applied for.

ISBN: 978-0-7534-6834-0

Printed in China
1 3 5 7 9 8 6 4 2
1TR/0512/UTD/WKT/140MA

Note to readers: the website addresses listed in this book are correct at the time of going to print. However, due to the ever-changing nature of the Internet, website addresses and content can change. Websites can contain links that are unsuitable for children. The publisher cannot be held responsible for changes in website addresses or content or for information obtained through a third party. We strongly advise that Internet searches are supervised by an adult.

Acknowledgments
The publisher would like to thank the following for permission to reproduce their material. Every care has been taken to trace copyright holders. However, if there have been unintentional omissions or failure to trace copyright holders, we apologize and will, if informed, endeavor to make corrections in any future edition.
b = bottom, *c* = center, *l* = left, *t* = top, *r* = right

Photographs: *cover* all images courtesy of Shutterstock.com; 1 Imagebank Getty; 2–3 A.&J. Verkalk Corbis; 4–5 Photonica Getty; 6*tr* Travelshots Alamy; 6*bl* Reportage Getty; 7 Don Mason Corbis; 8 Stone Getty; 9*tl* Nevada Weir Corbis; 9*r* Photolibrary.com; 10–11 Richard Cooke Alamy; 11*tl* Simon Fraser Science Photo Library; 12–13 Taxi Getty; 12*cr* Imagebank Getty; 12*bl* Photographer's Choice Getty; 14–15 Still Pictures; 15*tl* Still Pictures; 15*cr* Mike Greenslade Alamy; 16–17 Roy Morsch Zefa Corbis; 16 Photolibrary.com; 18–19 Taxi Getty; 18*b* Remi Benali Corbis; 19*tr* Photolibrary.com; 20–21 Photographer's Choice Getty; 21 Stockbyte Platinum Getty; 22 National Geographic Society Getty; 23 Still Pictures; 23*tr* Pekka Parviainen Science Photo Library; 24–25 Photolibrary.com; 25*tl* Stone Getty; 25*br* Still Pictures; 26 Stone + Getty; 27*tl* Jim Reed Corbis; 27 Rick Wilking Reuters Corbis; 28–29 Still Pictures; 29*tl* Still Pictures; 29*br* Iconica Getty; 30–31 Photographer's Choice Getty; 30*l* Photolibrary.com; 31 Iconica Getty; 32–33 Still Pictures; 33*t* Stone Getty; 33*b* Stone Getty; 34–35 Stone Getty; 35 Steve Bloom Alamy; 36–37 National Geographic Society Getty; 36*cr* Jim Reed Corbis; 36*bl* Masterfile; 38–39 Reportage Getty; 38*bl* Getty Editorial; 39*br* Corbis; 40 Keren Su Corbis; 41*tl* Still Pictures; 41*br* Zute Lightfoot Alamy; 48 Shutterstock Images/nadiya_sergey; 49*t* Shutterstock Images/Yuriy Poznuknov; 49*b* Shutterstock Images/Hector Conesa; 52*tr* Shutterstock Images/Yevgeniy Steshkin; 52*bl* Shutterstock Images/Graham Prentice; 53 Shutterstock Images/Hirurg; 56 Shutterstock Images/Jokerpro

Commissioned photography on pages 42–47 by Andy Crawford
Thank you to models Dilvinder Dilan Bhamra, Cherelle Clarke, Madeleine Roffey, and William Sartin

discover science

Weather

Caroline Harris

KINGFISHER
NEW YORK

Contents

What is weather?

Weather is all of the changes that happen in the air. Water, air, and heat from the Sun work together to make weather.

Warm and sunny

When the Sun is high up in the sky and there are not many clouds, the weather is hot and dry. If it is cloudy, the temperature is lower.

Let the rain fall

Without water, there would be no life on Earth. Rain helps plants grow and gives animals water to drink.

Icy water

Water freezes when it is very cold. This changes the weather. Snow falls instead of rain, and water on the ground turns to ice.

Our star

The Sun is a burning hot star. It is so bright that it lights up Earth. The Sun also helps make our weather. It heats the land and air to make the wind blow, and it warms the oceans to make clouds and rain.

Night and day

Earth spins around once every 24 hours. When one side of Earth faces the Sun, it is daytime there. On the other side of Earth, it is nighttime.

Sun worship

The Inca lived many years ago in South America. They worshiped the Sun. In those days, a lot of people thought that the Sun was a god because it was so powerful.

Burning heat

The Sun's rays can easily burn people's skin. Stay safe in the Sun by covering up and using sunscreen. Never look straight at the Sun.

Blanket of air

The atmosphere is a layer of air that covers Earth. It is where all weather happens. The atmosphere keeps our planet warm and protects it from danger, such as being hit by space rocks.

Blue skies

The sky looks blue on a clear day. This is because of the way sunlight shines through Earth's atmosphere.

Breathe in

The atmosphere is made up of a mixture of gases. Both plants and animals need these gases to live.

Up and away

The atmosphere has five layers. The one closest to Earth is the troposphere. This is where clouds form. The layer farthest from Earth is the exosphere.

Layers of the atmosphere

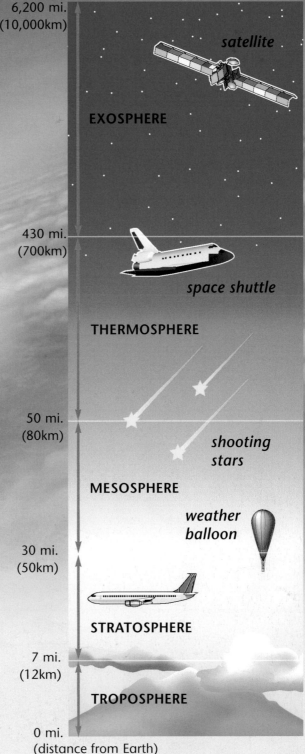

6,200 mi. (10,000km)

EXOSPHERE

satellite

430 mi. (700km)

space shuttle

THERMOSPHERE

50 mi. (80km)

shooting stars

MESOSPHERE

weather balloon

30 mi. (50km)

STRATOSPHERE

7 mi. (12km)

TROPOSPHERE

0 mi. (distance from Earth)

Changing seasons

Most countries have four seasons: winter, spring, summer, and fall. Seasons change because of the way Earth orbits the Sun. Each orbit takes one year.

Earth on the move

Earth tilts, so each pole is closer to the Sun and is warmer at different times of the year. When it is summer in the north, it is winter in the south.

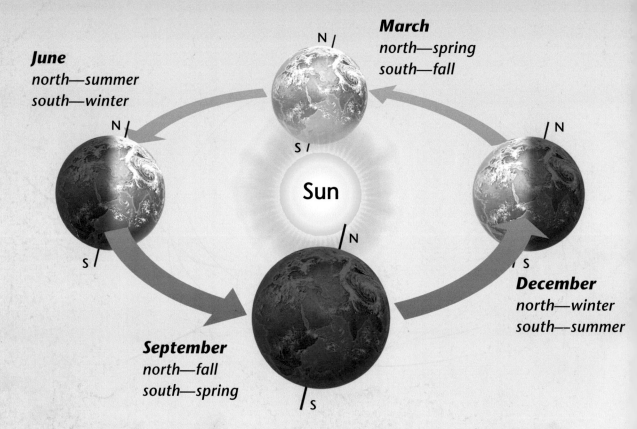

March
north—spring
south—fall

June
north—summer
south—winter

Sun

December
north—winter
south—summer

September
north—fall
south—spring

Spring and summer

In the spring, flowers bloom and many animals have babies. The warm weather of the summer follows the spring.

spring

Fall and winter

At the end of the summer, the fall arrives and the leaves fall off the trees. Then comes chilly winter.

fall

World climates

The normal weather in a place is called its climate. There are different types of climates around the world. Some are hot and dry, while others are freezing cold or warm and wet.

Icy cold
Antarctica has the coldest climate on Earth. The emperor penguins that live there have blubber and special feathers to help them stay warm.

Hot and dry

Deserts form where the climate is very dry and usually cloudless. They can change from sizzling hot during the day to freezing cold at night.

Warmed by the ocean

In Cornwall, U.K., there are palm trees, which usually grow only in hotter places. A warm ocean current makes the climate mild.

Blowing around

The air in the atmosphere is always on the move, blowing from one place to another. This is the wind. Some winds are only gentle breezes. Gales are strong winds that can blow tiles off roofs and people off their feet!

Weathervane
Whenever the wind blows a weathervane around, the arrow on it turns. The arrow stops once it points the way in which the wind is blowing.

Flying kites

People have been flying
kites for thousands of years.
The wind lifts the kite, and
the owner can pull or steer
it with a long string.

Wild winds

Strong winds can be very dangerous. They knock down buildings and injure people. But they are also useful— wind turbines can make electricity.

Dust storm

In places where the soil is dry, strong winds can make huge clouds of dust. These dust storms move quickly and can blow grit into eyes, clothes, and hair.

Twisting wind

A tornado is a spinning funnel of wind that comes from a storm cloud. Some tornadoes are so powerful that they can suck a house off the ground.

Whistling wind

The wind whistles when it blows hard through a small gap. It is the same as when someone whistles through their lips.

Blue planet

Water covers most of Earth. As the Sun warms oceans and lakes, it turns the water into vapor. Vapor is in the air, but it cannot be seen.

The water cycle

Water is always moving. When it rains, water runs into rivers, which flow into the ocean. From there, it turns into vapor and makes clouds. Then it rains again.

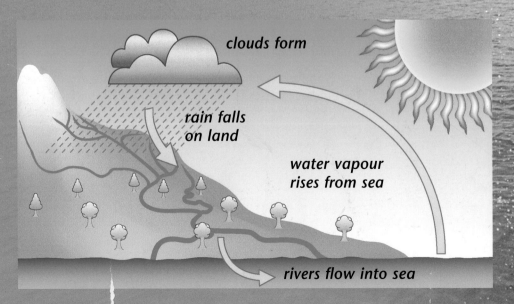

clouds form

rain falls on land

water vapour rises from sea

rivers flow into sea

Healthy water

Humans are also part of the water cycle. Mineral and tap water were once rain. People need to drink several glasses of water every day to stay healthy.

dolphins in the ocean

Enormous oceans

Oceans cover 72 percent of Earth's surface. They have a huge effect on our weather. Ocean currents carry with them warm, cold, or wet weather.

Mist and clouds

Clouds can be made from tiny
drops of water or from ice crystals.
They are formed when warm air
holding water vapor cools
down. Clouds come in
all shapes and sizes.

Fluffy cumulus

A cloud's name describes how
high up it is and what it looks
like. For example, the fluffy
clouds seen in warm weather
are called cumulus.

Glowing at night

Some clouds glow in the dark, just after sunset. They look bright blue and are crisscrossed with wavy lines.

Tiger in the mist

Mist and fog are clouds near the ground. They usually form in cool weather. This tiger's home in the jungle is very wet, so it is misty there even though it is warm.

Out in the rain

A raindrop is made when tiny drops of water in a cloud touch and join together. The raindrop gets larger and heavier, and finally it falls to the ground as rain.

The shape of rain

Rain may look like lines, but each raindrop is usually the shape of a sphere. Most are small— the size of a pencil tip.

Carried by the wind

Storms produce enormous, heavy raindrops. Strong winds keep the rain up in the air for a long time, so the drops get very big.

Leafy umbrella

Like humans, many animals like to shelter from the rain. Orangutans hold handfuls of leaves above their heads to stop getting wet.

Stormy days

A thunderstorm happens when clouds grow bigger and taller and gather more and more energy. Every day, there can be as many as 40,000 storms crashing down around the world.

Lightning strikes

Lightning is a spark of electricity that makes the air glow. It can move between clouds or shoot down to the ground onto trees or buildings.

High as a mountain

Thunderclouds can be enormous. In very severe storms, they can be taller than a mountain!

Hurricane damage

A hurricane is a group of thunderstorms that spin. At the center is a calm circle called the eye. When a hurricane hits land, it can cause a lot of damage.

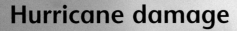

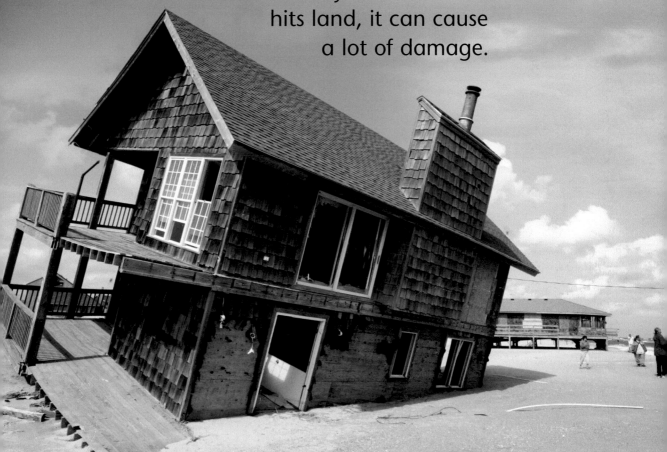

Wet and dry

Some parts of the world are rainy and wet. Other places are very dry. In deserts, years may pass without rainfall. But in the jungle, it can rain heavily all year long.

Pumping water
During a drought, there is not much rain. In very dry areas, people may have to walk to a well to get drinking water.

Water everywhere

When a lot of rain falls, it can cause floods. These are lakes of water that can cover a large area—even a whole city.

Dry earth

When it does not rain for a long time, the earth can become so dry and hard that it cracks.

Big freeze

When water gets very cold, it freezes into solid, slippery ice. You can see this as frost on plants and lawns or as the frozen hard layer on a pond.

Handful of ice
Hailstones are balls of ice made in thunderclouds. They fall like rain, and the largest ones can be the size of a grapefruit. Ouch!

Feathery crystals

Frost forms when air near the ground is wet and so cold that it freezes. When it is warmer, this wetness makes dew instead.

Mountains of ice

Ice weighs less than water. This is why huge icebergs float. But only a small part of the ice can be seen. The rest is hidden under the water.

Flakes of snow

Snowflakes are made from ice that forms high up in the clouds. In warm weather, the ice melts and falls to the ground as rain or sleet. If it is cold enough, it falls as snow.

Snowfall

Snowflakes are snow crystals that are stuck together. Big flakes form when it is just below freezing. This is when the crystals are stickiest.

Cozy snow

Snow can keep you warm!
The Inuit people, who live
in the Arctic, make
buildings called igloos
from blocks of snow.

Snow shapes

Most snow crystals have six sides,
but they never look exactly the
same as one another. They all form
different beautiful patterns.

Light shows

Sometimes, water and ice crystals can make light look very colorful or unusual. They can cause amazing effects, such as sundogs and the beautiful glowing light of a rainbow.

Colorful rainbow

When it rains and is sunny at the same time, it is sometimes possible to see a rainbow. A rainbow is especially clear if a dark cloud lies behind the rain.

Sundogs

The two lights on each side of the Sun are called sundogs. They happen when sunlight shines through ice crystals in a particular way. The lights follow the Sun like a dog follows its owner.

Extreme weather

Sometimes, weather can be wild and dangerous. Extreme weather can cause storms, floods, wildfires, and droughts.

Waterpower

Floods may stretch over huge distances and cause a lot of damage. They can leave people stranded so that they need to be rescued by helicopter or boat.

Fighting fires

Wildfires break out in hot weather. This is because trees and plants dry out and then burn easily.

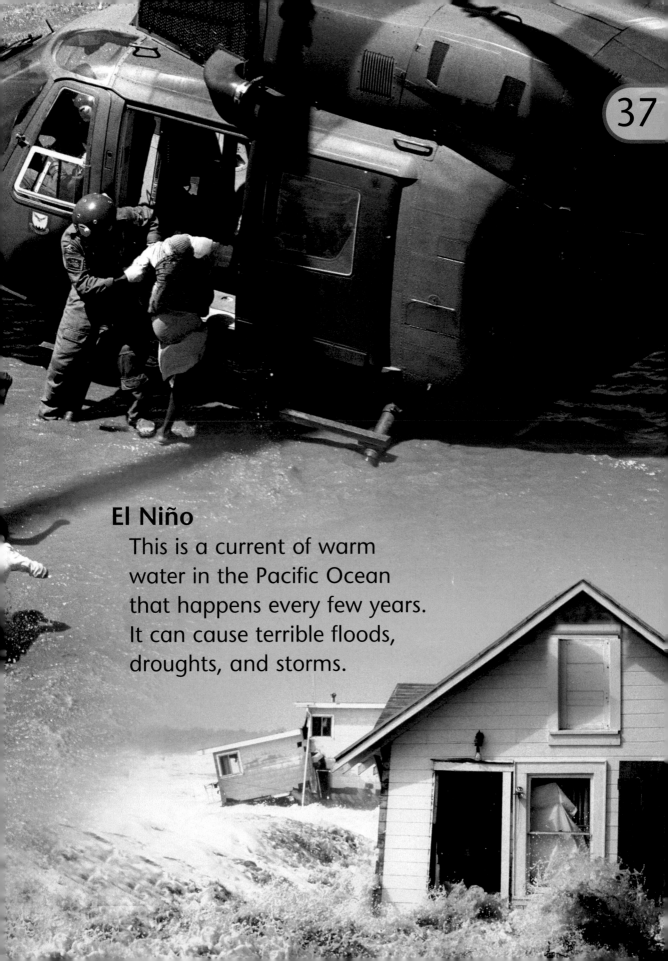

El Niño

This is a current of warm
water in the Pacific Ocean
that happens every few years.
It can cause terrible floods,
droughts, and storms.

38 Rain or shine?

Weather forecasts tell us what the weather will be like for the next few days. Scientists use instruments and computers to make these forecasts.

Storm spotting

Trucks with radar can find storms that are far away. Scientists then follow the storms and measure their strength.

Damp seaweed

There are easy ways of forecasting weather. For example, seaweed gets fat and floppy in wet air. This might mean that rain is coming.

Weather balloons
Scientists use balloons to lift instruments high up into the sky. These then measure the weather.

Future weather

Earth's climate naturally goes through times when it is a lot warmer or icier than it is today. However, many scientists believe that humans are changing the weather.

Smoky cars

The weather may be changing because of pollution. It traps too much of the Sun's heat. This heat would normally escape into outer space.

Getting warmer

Earth's climate is heating up. This makes ice melt and break away from icebergs and glaciers. As a result, the levels of the oceans rise and flood areas of land.

elp for farmers

Scientists are now better at forecasting weather several months ahead. Farmers use these forecasts to help them decide which crops to plant each year.

Riding the wind

Making a kite

Kites soar in the sky because
the wind pushes them upward.
Decorate your kite with an animal
face—try a tiger!

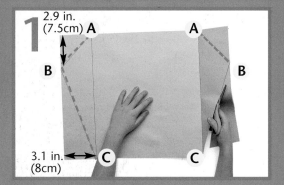

Following the measurements shown
above, draw lines between A and
C, A and B, and B and C. Cut the
paper from C to B and then B to A.

You will need:

- Scissors
- Sheet of 11x17 in. (A3) paper
- Pencil
- Ruler
- Markers
- Tape
- Hole punch
- 2 long drinking straws
- Colored tissue paper
- Thin cotton string
- Thin stick

Turn the paper over and decorate
your kite. You could draw a tiger.
Make sure A is at the top of the
kite and C is at the bottom.

Put tape on the corners of the
paper at B. Then use the hole
punch to make holes through
the tape 1 in. (2.5cm) from
the edge, at B.

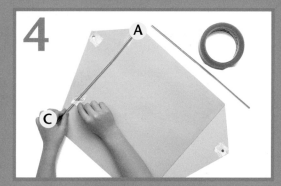

Turn the kite over. Use the tape to fasten the straws on both sides of the paper along the lines between A and C.

Using the scissors, cut strips of colored tissue paper 8 in. (20cm) long. Tape the strips along the bottom edge of the kite.

Now your kite is ready to fly! Take a trip to a park and ask an adult to throw the kite high up into the air. Pull it along, holding tightly onto the stick.

Thread 30 in. (80cm) of string through the punched-out holes and tie the ends together. The sides of the kite should slightly bend inwards. Wind another long piece of string onto the stick. Tie the end to the middle of the string on the kite.

Sun catcher

Flashing lights

Your sun catcher will sparkle in the sunlight. If you place it near fruit bushes, it can help scare away birds and stop them from eating the berries.

Place two CDs on paper with the shiny sides facing down. Spread on glue. Stick the CDs together. Leave to dry. Repeat with the other CDs.

You will need:
- 6 blank CDs
- Glue for plastic/paper
- Shiny cardboard
- Pencil
- Scissors
- Thread (6x8 in. (20cm),2x10 in. (25cm), 1x14 in. (35cm))
- String (14 in. (35cm))
- Small bells
- Stick (10 in. (25cm))

Draw six moons and six stars on the cardboard. Cut them out. Glue two star shapes together, shiny sides out. Repeat with all shapes.

Ask an adult to make a small hole in the point of each star and moon. Poke 8 in. (20cm) of thread into each hole and pull it halfway through.

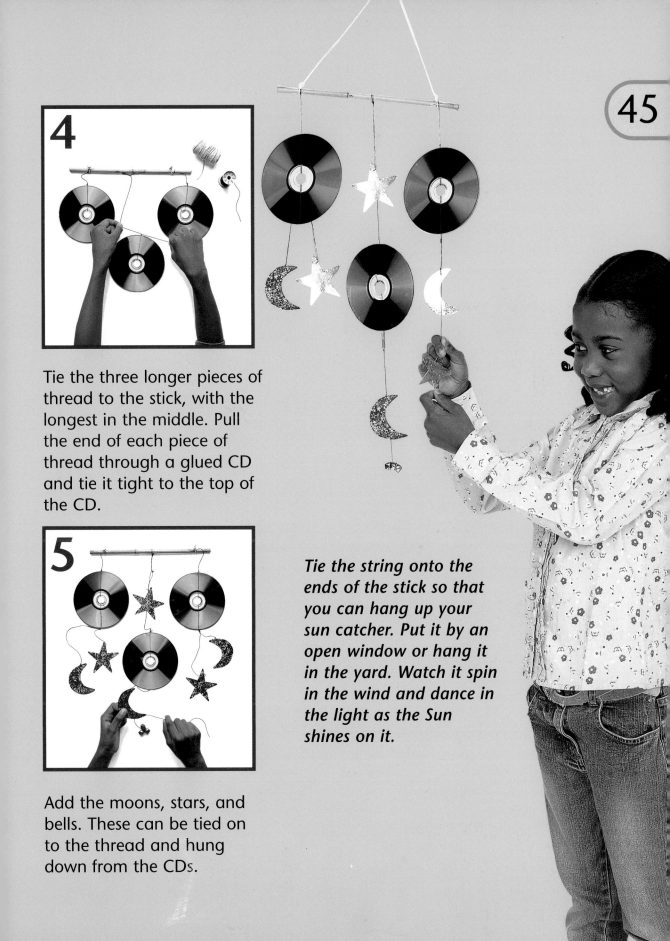

4

Tie the three longer pieces of thread to the stick, with the longest in the middle. Pull the end of each piece of thread through a glued CD and tie it tight to the top of the CD.

5

Add the moons, stars, and bells. These can be tied on to the thread and hung down from the CDs.

Tie the string onto the ends of the stick so that you can hang up your sun catcher. Put it by an open window or hang it in the yard. Watch it spin in the wind and dance in the light as the Sun shines on it.

Creating colors

Make a rainbow
See how water is able to split light into different colors to make an amazing rainbow in your home.

You will need:
- Glass container
- Small mirror
- Flashlight
- Water pitcher

Place the glass container on a table in a room with plain, light walls. Use the pitcher to half fill the container with warm water.

Put the mirror in the container and slightly tilt it upward. Close the curtains and turn off the lights so that the room is very dark.

rainbow

Shine the flashlight onto the mirror and a rainbow should appear on the wall.

Swirling winds

Make a tornado

The swirling water in this
experiment acts in the
same way as the spinning
winds of a wild tornado.

You will need:
- Big plastic bottle with cap
- Dishwashing liquid
- Food coloring
- Glitter

1

Fill the bottle with water and add
three drops of dishwashing liquid
and some food coloring. Shake in
some glitter, which will act like
the dust that a tornado picks up.

*Tightly screw the cap back
on and then swirl your
bottle around in circles.
Quickly put it down and
watch what happens.*

tornado

Glossary

Arctic—the area around the North Pole

blubber—a layer of fat

breeze—a gentle, light wind

crystal—a substance or mineral found in nature that has formed into a regular shape

current—a river of warmer or cooler water in an ocean

cycle—events that happen again and again in the same order

dew—drops of water that form on grass and other surfaces when vapor in the air cools

drought—a long period of time without rain

effect—a result

energy—power and force

extreme—most unusual or severe

fog—a thick cloud of tiny water droplets in the atmosphere

freeze—to turn to ice

frost—small white ice crystals that form on the ground when the temperature falls below freezing

funnel—a tube shape with a wider top and narrower bottom

gas—a shapeless substance, such as air, that is not solid or liquid

glacier—a solid river of ice

instrument—a tool used to take measurements

jungle—a hot, wet place full of trees and plants

mineral water—water found in nature, often bottled and sold as drinking water

ocean—a very large area of water

orbit—to move in a complete circle around a star or planet

pole—the point farthest north or farthest south on a planet

pollution—harmful dirt, such as exhaust fumes from cars

produce—to make

radar—an instrument that can locate objects far away by bouncing sounds off them

sphere—a ball shape

star—a large ball of burning gas in space that appears as a point of light in the night sky

temperature—how hot or cold it is

vapor—tiny drops of water in the air that look like mist

well—a deep hole that leads to water under the ground

wildfire—a fire in a forest or grassland

wind turbine—a machine that turns in the wind to make electricity

worship—to show something, or someone, love or respect by praying, chanting, or singing

ray—a beam of light that travels in a straight line

severe—strong and powerful

shelter—to protect from bad weather or danger

sleet—rain mixed with snow or hail

solid—not a liquid or a gas

Parent and teacher notes

The content of this book will be useful to help teach and reinforce various elements of the science and language arts curricula in the elementary grades. It also provides opportunities for crosscurricular lessons in math, geography, and art.

Extension activities

Writing
Which season is your favorite? Write one or two pages describing some of the things you like best about that season, including your favorite activities at that time of the year.

Writen and oral language
Choose a type of severe weather, such as a hurricane or tornado, that you find particularly interesting. Research to find out more about it and write a one- or two-page report. Illustrate it with pictures from magazines or newspapers, or with your own artwork. Give a five-minute report to share what you have learned.

Creative writing
Imagine that you are out in the woods when you realize that a storm is approaching. What do you do? Where do you go? What happens? Write a story about your imaginary experience.

Science
The study of weather relates to the scientific themes of weather and climate and Earth science.

Some specific links to the science curriculum include astronomy (pp. 8–9, 10–11); atmosphere (pp. 10–11); climate change (pp. 40–41); clouds (pp. 22–23); seasons (pp. 12–13); severe weather and natural disasters (pp. 18–19, 26–27, 28–29, 36–37); and technology (pp. 38–39).

Crosscurricular links
Math/graphing
What types of weather are typical at different times of year where you live? Make a graph or chart to keep track of the number of sunny days, wind, rain, etc., in

each month. A single day might include more than one thing to record on your graph!

Writing and art
Research to find the names of different types of clouds, beginning with page 22. Create an illustrated cloud dictionary with a page about each type of cloud.

Geography
Read the newspaper or look online for information about severe weather and/or natural disasters that are happening or have happened recently in different parts of the world. Find each location on a world map and mark it with a symbol representing the type of weather event and the date. Keep your map updated for several weeks or even months.

Using the projects
Children can do these projects at home. Here are some ideas for extending them:

Pages 42–43: Kites can also be made out of newspaper, plastic garbage bags, and other materials. Look for directions on the Internet or in a book about making kites. Make and fly some different types of kites. How do they compare?

Pages 44–45: The sparkle of the sun catcher is caused by sunlight being reflected from the shiny surfaces. What other objects can you find that reflect sunlight? Create a second sun catcher using small shiny objects that you have found or put together.

Pages 46–47: Look for small rainbows in places where the Sun shines through water or certain objects at the right angle. You might find them near an aquarium or fish bowl, on a surface near a crystal or glass object in a sunny spot, such as a window, or even in the fan of water when a hose is sprayed out into the sunlight.

Did you know?

- Without the weather to spread the Sun's heat around the world, the central areas of the planet would get hotter and hotter and the poles colder and colder. Nothing would be able to live on Earth.

- Roy Cleveland Sullivan was a park ranger in Shenandoah National Park in Virginia. Between 1942 and 1977, Sullivan was hit by lightning on an incredible seven different occasions and survived all of them. He lost his big toenail in 1942, his eyebrows in 1969, and had his hair set on fire twice.

- To see a rainbow, you must have your back to the Sun. Sometimes, double rainbows can form. In the second bow, the colors are always ordered the opposite way.

- A lightning bolt generates temperatures five times hotter than the 11,000°F (6,000°C) found at the surface of the Sun.

- Mawsynram is a village in northeastern India. It is the wettest place on Earth, with an average annual rainfall of 475 in. (11,872mm). Most of it falls during the monsoon season.

- The Atacama Desert in Chile is one of the driest places in the world. To obtain drinking water, Chileans have set up fog catchers that look like giant volleyball nets. The water in ocean fog sticks to the nets and is collected.

- The largest types of clouds are known as cumulonimbus clouds, and they contain huge amounts of water. The clouds reach a height of 11 mi. (18km), which is twice as high as Mount Everest.

- On August 6, 2000, a shower of fish fell in Great Yarmouth, Norfolk, England. Sometimes, strong winds during a thunder-storm can scoop up fish and frogs from rivers or the ocean. The animals are carried along in the clouds and later fall like rain!

- At the center of a tornado, winds can reach up to 370 miles (600km) per hour, making them the fastest winds on Earth. A tornado leapfrogs across the land, causing great damage. It can destroy one house and leave the house next door untouched.

- A tiny drop of water will stay in Earth's atmosphere for an average of 11 days. If all of the water in the air fell at the same time, it could cover the whole planet with 1 in. (25mm) of rain.

- The largest hailstone ever recorded fell on July 23, 2010 in Vivian, South Dakota. It measured 8 in. (20cm) in diameter—the size of a bowling ball!

- The lowest world temperature ever recorded was a bitter −123°F (−89.6°C) at Vostok Station, Antarctica, on July 21, 1983.

- The greatest snowfall ever recorded was on Mount Rainier, Washington, in 1972, when more than 98 ft. (30m) of snow fell in one winter.

Weather quiz

The answers to these questions can all be found by looking back through the book. See how many you get right. You can check your answers on page 56.

1) How long does it take for Earth to orbit the Sun?
   A—A day
   B—A month
   C—A year

2) Which layer of Earth's atmosphere is closest to the ground?
   A—Mesosphere
   B—Exosphere
   C—Troposphere

3) Which continent has the coldest climate on Earth?
   A—Asia
   B—Antarctica
   C—Oceania

4) When water is warmed, what does it turn into first?
   A—Vapor
   B—Cloud
   C—Mist

5) What is the center of a hurricane called?
   A—Ear
   B—Eye
   C—Nose

6) Which of these statements is not true?
   A—Ice weighs less than water.
   B—Icebergs float.
   C—Only a small part of an iceberg is under the water.

7) Where do droughts often occur?
   A—In deserts
   B—In mountains
   C—In jungles

8) How many sides does a snow crystal usually have?
   A—Six
   B—Seven
   C—Eight

9) Which of these is a current of warm water in the Pacific Ocean?
   A—El Dorado
   B—El Niño
   C—El Greco

10) What happens to seaweed when it is about to rain?
    A—It gets fat.
    B—It dries out.
    C—It changes color.

11) What is a powerful spinning wind called?
    A—Tornado
    B—Turbine
    C—Cumulus

12) Lightning is a spark of what?
    A—Ice
    B—Electricity
    C—Gas

Find out more

Books to read

Can Lightning Strike the Same Place Twice? And Other Questions About Earth, Weather, and the Environment (Is that a Fact?) by Joanne Mattern, Lerner, 2010

Climate Change Catastrophe (Can the Earth Survive?) by Richard Spilsbury, Rosen Central, 2010

Earth's Weather and Climate (Planet Earth) by Jim Pipe, Gareth Stevens, 2008

Experiments with Weather and Climate (Cool Science) by John Bassett, Gareth Stevens, 2010

Explorers: Weather by Deborah Chancellor, Kingfisher, 2012

Lightning, Hurricanes, and Blizzards: The Science of Storms (WeatherWise) by Paul Fleisher, Lerner, 2011

Places to visit

Rochester Museum and Science Center, New York
www.rmsc.org
This museum has lots of hands-on exhibits. Lightning flashes, thunder crashes, and mist rises as you enter the weather gallery. You will find out where clouds come from, why it rains, and what causes lightning. In the weather studio, you can use a computer to present your own weather forecast!

Orlando Science Center, Florida
www.osc.org
The weather center in this museum gives you the chance to do a weather report in front of a screen just like the pros. First you will learn how the weather works—from rainbows to tornadoes, and then you can use the forecasting equipment located on the roof of the museum!

The Weather Museum, Houston, Texas
www.wxresearch.org/wpmuseum
Visitors to this museum can experience what it is like to walk through a tornado, or be in the middle of a hurricane! Other interactive exhibits include a computer-generated lighting display, a cloud chamber, and a landscape where you can change the terrain to see how flash floods form.

Websites

http://eo.ucar.edu/webweather/cloud3.html
Find out about the different types of clouds and test your knowledge with some interactive games.

www.scholastic.com/kids/weather
Use this interactive weather maker to create the weather of your choice. You can make it snowy, windy, sunny, or rainy.

www.miamisci.org/hurricane/weathertools.html
This site shows you how to make tools for your own weather station.

www.weatherwizkids.com
All the different types of weather are explained on this website for kids. It also has lots of weather experiments to try out.

Weather quiz answers

1) C	7) A
2) C	8) A
3) B	9) B
4) A	10) A
5) B	11) A
6) C	12) B